"THE DIVINE SECRET SOCIETY"

MANY ARE CALLED
FEW ARE CHOSEN

RICHARD L. HANDS

WESTBOW
PRESS®
A DIVISION OF THOMAS NELSON
& ZONDERVAN

WestBow Press books may be ordered through booksellers or by contacting:

WestBow Press
A Division of Thomas Nelson & Zondervan
1663 Liberty Drive
Bloomington, IN 47403
www.westbowpress.com
844-714-3454

Because of the dynamic nature of the Internet, any web addresses or
links contained in this book may have changed since publication and
may no longer be valid. The views expressed in this work are solely those
of the author and do not necessarily reflect the views of the publisher,
and the publisher hereby disclaims any responsibility for them.

Any people depicted in stock imagery provided by Getty Images are
models, and such images are being used for illustrative purposes only.
Certain stock imagery © Getty Images.

Scripture quotations are from the Holy Bible, King James Version
(Authorized Version). First published in 1611. Quoted from the KJV Classic
Reference Bible, Copyright © 1983 by The Zondervan Corporation.

ISBN: 978-1-6642-9691-6 (sc)
ISBN: 978-1-6642-9692-3 (e)

Library of Congress Control Number: 2023906753

Print information available on the last page.

WestBow Press rev. date: 04/10/2023

CONTENTS

INTRODUCTION

THE HOLY SPIRIT REVEALS THE MYSTERIES OF GOD
ONLY TO THOSE OF THE DIVINE SECRET SOCIETY.
MORE BOOKS WILL BE WRITTEN PROVIDING
BIBLICAL INFORMATION TO HELP AID THE CHOSEN
GENERATION (I PETER 2:9) THAT HAS RECEIVED
REVELATION OF WISDOM OF HIS DIVINE WORDS (I
COR 28:19)

> Which things also we speak, not in the word
> which man's wisdom teacheth,
> but which the Holy Ghost teacheth;
> comparing spiritual things with
> spiritual. (I Corinthians 2:13)

ORDINARY CONVERT

I CORINTHIANS 1:26 FOR YE SEE YOUR CALLING, BRETHREN, HOW THAT NOT MANY WISE MEN AFTER THE FLESH, NOT MANY MIGHTY, NOT MANY NOBLE, ARE CALLED: (KJV). **...I do nothing of myself; but as my Father hath taught me, I speak these things (John 8:28).**

This verse shows how God can call on whom he choose to do and perform his work through. Many called by God doubted their abilities meaning the person to the world standards may not seem to have the best requirements to fill the position of calling in their eye. BUT GOD HATH CHOSEN THE FOOLISH THINGS OF THE WORLD TO CONFOUND THE WISE; AND GOD HATH CHOSEN THE WEAK THINGS OF THE WORLD TO CONFOUND THE THINGS WHICH ARE MIGHTY; I CORINTHIANS 1:27 (KJV). As God has mentioned before his ways is not our ways, the natural (carnal) man picks and choose by ones' worldly status or appearance, While the God of divine sprit makes his pick by one spirit. Not considering things that the world (Worldly minded) take heed to AND BASE THINGS OF THE WORLD, AND THINGS WHICH ARE DEPISED, HATH GOD CHOSEN, YEA, AND THINGS WHICH ARE NOT, TO BRING TO NOUGHT THINGS THAT ARE: 1COR: 1:28(KJV) THAT NO FLESH SHOULD GLORY IN HIS PERSENCE 1COR: 1:29(KJV). Where we lack strength many times God works his will through us, leaving us knowing the task at hand performed was only through his divine actions, not of the flesh like he proven in all that was called and chosen by him. In return each person from kings to shepherds came to know the glory is in God not ones' self. So there are no excuses when you hear the Holy Spirit speaking to your spirit, you reading this book are not by your worldly choice or a mistake. God has proven all through the bible there is a purpose for everything and the purpose of you reading this book is the beginning of your commission (calling) his will and purpose for your life. Lets start by knowing your calling.

KNOWING YOUR CALLING

Knowing your calling is a destiny that was birthed before you were conceived in the womb. A spiritual birth took place when GOD conceived and formed your soul to be a part of his kingdom. Each one of us is a part of the body that Jesus speaks of that shapes GOD kingdom (Roman 12: 4-7), Everyone has a divine (GOD Given) part to partake of in the body (GOD KINGDOM), that is to add growth and function as a whole to fulfill the will of GOD and plan for his chosen generation (THIS IS YOU). No matter the story of your past The Heavenly Father is concern for your future. GOD knows the great things he has in stored for you in his DIVINE KINGDOM. **BUT YE ARE A CHOSEN GENERATION, A ROYAL PRIESTHOOD, AN HOLY NATION, A PECULIAR PEOPLE; THAT YE SHOULD SHOW FORTH PRAISE OF HIM WHO HATH CALLED YOU OUT OF DARKNESS INTO HIS MARVELOUS LIGHT: (I PETER 2:9) (KJV).** GOD called you out of your death (SIN) to give you a new life and beginning (KEYS TO ENTER GODS KINGDOM). JESUS said that he went to prepare a place for us, knowing GOD wish that no one perish. WHICH IN TIME PAST WERE NOT A PEOPLE, BUT ARE NOW THE PEOPLE OF GOD WHICH HAD NOT OBTAINED MERCY, BUT NOW HAVE OBTAINED MERCY (1 PETER 2: 10) (KJV). Where no one soul should be casted into

Hades (The Gates of Hell), but written in THE BOOK OF LIFE. By saving ones' soul it not only benefit you, but those around you and most of all the body (GODS KINGDOM). Knowing your calling is truly knowing who you are (**YOUR TRUE EXISTENCE**). GOD allows THE HOLY GHOST to nurture your soul, which allows your step to lead you into calling guidance of the HOLY SPIRIT. Everyone commission (calling) GOD has assigned may carry different responsibilities, but that do not mean one calling is more important than the other. Just like the human body the brain is the biggest human muscle, and has a lot of responsibilities. But the body depends on the toes to help the body balance, walk and run. The brain alone cannot do these actions properly, without both working together. This is why everyone must take heed and walk in their personal calling to help the body (GOD KINGDOM). Coming together and working as one (A WHOLE). I BIND any spirit of self-doubt, insecurity and fear and LOOSE it in HEAVEN that may try to hinder your soul,

(**Spiritual Warfare/ talked about in the chapter titled Opposition**) telling lies you are not what and who GOD said you are. A deceptive voice Satan speaks to your soul to manipulate and weaken the divine calling for your spirit. The Liar (meaning of the name Satan) can only speak through lies, and his legion of demons (satanic spirits) on terms of spirits in the natural realm. Satan strategies to stop you from strengthen The Body (God Divine Kingdom). This is why understanding Spiritual Warfare is a must to arm you properly in the battlefield. Opposition is a frontline weapon hidden like bombs in a minefield, pay attention to Satan and your every move.

OPPOSITION

OPPOSITION IS JUST A SURE SIGN YOU ARE THE LORD CHILD (CHOSEN ONE), WITH A CALLING ONLY YOU CAN BRING TO LIGHT. A WAR OF SATANIC DARKNESS

AND DIVINE LIGHT SPIRITUAL WARFARE, YOU ARE TO BE A SOLIDER IN TRAINING SO LETS BEGIN. (Luke 9: 23, 27)

OPPOSITION comes in many different forms and directions when you are at the breakthrough of your calling, it can be on a personal level or professional one. Satan has studied you to learn your strengths and weakness. **Satan** (THE ADVERSARY) knowing this is a spiritual battle and like any army going to war you must study your opponent to correctly set up a defense and counter attack. A strong defense that withstand can only be built starting with a strong **DIVINE SPIRITUAL FONDATION.** Allowing your soul to be filled with the HOLY GHOST, and God given guidance and wisdom of the HOLY SPIRIT. You must know your adversary and his weapons of choice THE KINGDOM OF GOD IS AT HAND. So allow the leadership of the HOLYSPIRIT to be a compass to and on the spiritual battlefield.

(I will instruct thee and teach thee in the way which thou shalt go: I will guide thee with mine eye. Psalms 32:8)

CASUALITIES OF WAR

Now you have entered the battlefield **you must die** in order to win. Not like other battles to stay alive is a method of winning, but death to ones' self is key in the spirit of spiritual warfare. To have the strength like Samson, David and Joshua had over their enemies, in order to bind up the on battlefield and loose him in heaven

(IN THE HAND OF GOD)

Judges 15: 14,15 (The power of the Lord on Samson at battle)
And when he came unto Lehi, the Philistines shouted against him, and the spirit of the Lord came mightily upon him (Samson), and the cords that were upon his arms became as flax that was burnt with fire, and his bands loosed from off his hands

(Judges 15:14). **And he (Samson) found a new jawbone of an ass, and put forth his hand, and took it, and slew a thousand men therewith (Judges 15:15). This verse shows that the Lord can be with you spiritually and in the natural while facing a battle in life, as he were with David, Joshua and his chosen generations then and now.**

GETHSEMANE

For we wrestle not against flesh and blood, but against principalities, against the rulers of darkness of this world, against spiritual wickedness in high places (Ephesians 6: 12 KJV). Wherefore take unto you the whole armour of GOD that ye may be able to withstand in the evil day, and having done all, to stand (Ephesians 6:13 KJV). At your point of entering divinity Satan sends satanic forces of his spirit like to distract and hinder your walk with God causing derailment from your God given course. Many times Satan uses discomfort of the flesh to cloud our focus in the spirit, which is why we must die in the flesh to live clearly in Divine Spirit. Satan also has spirits he tries to send to you (The Flesh) in order for his will to be done against the will of our Heavenly Father. Worldly enticement, advances, or set backs are some of the satanic spirits used by Satan, more depending on the person like they say pick your poison. The few mentioned and others to come can be overcome by your Divine Spirit, but in the spirit not the flesh like Jesus said.

And he said, Abba, Father, all things are possible unto thee; take away this cup from me: nevertheless not what I will, but what thou wilt (Mark 14:36 KJV).

(The cup Jesus talks about is the crucifixion of the flesh (which is of our sinful nature) he knew the pain to endure of the flesh (The discomfort you experience when falling in to the will of God the crucifixion begins) but he quickly rebuked it (The flesh), it being a tool of the will of Satan instead of Jesus divine will from God.

The spirit is willing but the flesh is weak (Mark 14:38)

Protection by The Flesh

Then said Jesus unto him, put up again thy sword into his place: for all they that take the sword shall perish with the sword (Matthew 26:52 KJV). In Jesus last hours he tells his disciples you cannot form a defense by ways of the flesh as man may think this brings death, a false defense. Only a Divine spirit God has for his chosen can provide indestructible protection. Jesus said, Thinkest thou that I cannot now pray to my Father, and he shall presently give me more than twelve legions of angels (Matthew 26:53 KJV)? Jesus is speaking of The Holy Spirit (Divine Spirit) as he prays that God hears and react to. While acts of the flesh falls on dead ears (No Protection of God not of his will) an action of your will (The Flesh). Jesus also asked his disciples, But how then shall the scriptures be fulfilled, that thus it must be? (Matthew 26:54 KJV). Jesus is showing how it is always about God will for your life, everyone life partake in God Holy scriptures that is why you must take heed to your calling

(As part of the Body/ God kingdom), so as Jesus said the scriptures be fulfilled.

OUR FLESH HAS A SELF DESTRUCTIVE NATURE. Warring against ones' own self, referring to the spirit that dwells in it which gives life (Roman 8:12,15). The first and best weapon of Satan is our own flesh that main objective is to cater to it's own worldly lust and desires. The Lord grants us a free will because how much he loves us, but the flesh is self-centered and tries to demand a will for your life. Jesus also felt the will of Satan (The Flesh), but quickly rebuked it as he prayed the prayer in GETHSEMANE hours before his flesh would be crucified (put to death) for our sins of the flesh. Satan tried to make him give in to his flesh to not be led to the cross (And they that are Christ's have crucified the flesh with the affections and lusts. Galatians 5: 24/ victorious), knowing if Jesus gave in to the flesh the will of God would not come to pass at that given time through him. That is the same plan Satan use to stop God divine will for you that only you can bring forth (that is your assigned commission). Victory on the battlefield is in your assignment, vise versa defeat when you don't know Satan war tactic is death to the spirit by ways of giving in to the flesh.

Satan weapons of destruction

Now the works of the flesh are manifest, which are these; adultery, fornication, uncleanness, lasciviousness, idolatry, witchcraft, hatred, variance, emulations, wrath, strife, seditions, heresies, envyings, murders, drunkenness, revelings, and such like: of the which I tell you before, as I have also told you in time past, that they which do such things shall not inherit the kingdom of God (Galatians 5: 19,21 KJV).

Just naming a few...

40 days 40 nights on the battlefield

...Walk in the spirit, and ye shall not fulfill the lust of the flesh. For the flesh lusteth (spiritual warfare) against the spirit, and the spirit against the flesh: (Galatians 5:16,17)

Jesus of the divine spirit, fought with the flesh. Satan tried to uplift Jesus during an intense self-denial (The Flesh) stage of spiritual warfare. The scriptures show a carbon copy of some of the ways he tries to satisfy the flesh in order to deaden your Divine Spirit. Causing you to lose focus and be led into a sneak attack on your soul. Lets look at 40 days 40 nights Satan battle plan.

And straightway coming up out of the water, he saw the heavens opened, and the Spirit like a dove descending upon him: (Mark 1:10). And there came a voice from heaven, saying Thou art my beloved Son, in whom I am well pleased (Mark 1:11). And immediately the Spirit driveth him into the wilderness (Mark 1:12). And he was there in the wilderness forty days, tempted of

Satan; and was with the wild beasts; and the angels ministered unto him (Mark 1: 13).

Getting to know (The Adversary) prepare for battle

And when he had fasted forty days and forty nights, he was afterward an hungered (Matthew 4:2). And when the tempter came to him, he said, If thou be the Son of God, command that these stones be made bread (Matthew 4:3). But he answered and said, It is written, Man shall not live by bread alone, but by every word that proceedeth out of the mouth of God (Matthew 4:4). Then the devil taketh him up into the holy city, and setteh him on a pinnacle of temple, (Matthew 4:5). And saith unto him, If thou be the Son of God, cast thyself down: for it is written, He shall give his angels charge concerning thee: and in their hands they shall bear thee up, lest at any time thou dash thy foot against a stone (Matthew 4:6). Jesus said unto him, It is written again, Thou shalt not tempt the Lord thy God (Matthew 4:7). Again, the devil taketh him up into an exceeding high mountain, and showeth him all the kingdoms of the world, and the glory of them; (Matthew 4:8). And saith unto him, All these things will I give thee, if thou wilt fall down and worship me (Matthew 4:9). Then saith Jesus unto him, Get thee hence, Satan: for it is written, Thou shalt worship the Lord thy God, and him only shalt thou serve (Matthew 4:10). Then the devil leaveth him, and behold, angels came and ministered unto him (Matthew 4:11).

The testing before the Blessing

The Lord always leads his chosen ones into some kind of wilderness stage (training for battle/spiritual warfare). While in the wilderness you are tried and pressured like coal that later produces a diamond, by nature of pressure. This form a divine training strengthens you as a whole, mainly in areas of faith and patience. In the way your wilderness come may differ from others, but you know when you have entered it because the Lord spirit will be a voice in your spirit. The spirit of the Lord will be in you, beyond what the flesh (Satan) will try to make feel and believe. At this time the Lord is providing you with divine skills to be able to stand strong against the battle ways of the adversary, while keeping his commandments. This was told to the Children of Israel (a chosen generation of mixed ethnic groups) when they were about to enter their wilderness stage to be trained and tested for 40 years. The Lord says... All the commandments which I command thee this day shall ye observe to do, that ye may live, and multiply, and go in and possess the land which the Lord sware unto your fathers (Deuteronomy 8:1). And thou shalt remember all the way which the Lord thy God led thee these forty years in the wilderness, to humble thee, and to prove thee, to know what was in thine heart, whether thou wouldest keep his commandments, or no (Deuteronomy 8:2). The remembrance the Lord speaks of is how he would be your Jehovah-jierh (provider during trials and tribulations), which also tests your faith in him (faith builder). Building faith in the Lord ways not man ways (The Flesh) allows the Holy Spirit to keep you within the Lord commandments. Without faith in the Lord you start to believe in works of the flesh that is why... And he humbled thee, and suffered thee to hunger, and fed thee manna, which thou knewest not, neither did thy fathers know; that he might make thee know that man doth not live by bread only, but by every word that proceedeth out of the mouth of the Lord doth man live (Deuteronomy 8:3). Whatever opposition you may face during your journey to your Divine Calling "The promise of the Lord" is never to leave you despite of what the flesh see in sight or feels. They felt hunger, but by the hand of the Lord in order to show he is the chosen ones (Divine generation/ You) Jehovah-jierh (provider) feeding them manna (In the bible known as angel food). Food became limited and no man could bring forth food, so the Lord allowed them to receive the manna from heaven for food, letting it be known it was divinely given by the heavenly father keeping his word to tend to their needs.

Thy raiment waxed not old upon thee, neither did thy foot swell, these forty years (Deuteronomy 8:4). The Lord even made sure their clothes did not turn to rags during the 40 years or feet swell, proving the Lord will up hold you in every way during opposition on the way to your commission (Divine Calling).

Crucify The Flesh

For whosoever will save his life shall lose it: And whosoever will lose his life for my sake shall find it (Matthew 16:24-26 KJV). Therefore, brethren, we are debtors, not to the flesh, to live after the flesh. For if ye live after the flesh, ye shall die: but if ye through the spirit do mortify the deeds of the body, ye shall live (Romans 8:12,13).

Protection

There shall no evil befall thee, Neither shall any plague come nigh thy dwelling. For he shall give his angels charge over thee, to keep thee in all thy ways (Psalms 91:10,11 / Genesis 19:15). Behold, God will not cast away a perfect man, neither will he help the evildoers: (Job 8:20,21). The Lord also will be a refuge for the oppressed, a refuge in times of trouble (Psalms 9:9). The eternal God is thy refuge, and underneath are the everlasting arms: and he shall thrust out the enemy from before thee; and shall say, destroy them (Deuteronomy 33:27). The spirit is strengthened in battle by taking on the whole armour of GOD (Ephesian 6:14).

STAND BOLD

And for me, that utterance may be given unto me, that I may open my mouth boldly, to make known the mystery of the gospel (Ephesian 6:19).

FEAR NOT

Are you still in doubt? Doubting what and who you are in the body of the Divine Kingdom. You should be if you are still examining your weakness and flaws. You are looking at what your limits are instead of saying; I can do all things through Christ which strengtheneth me (Philippians 4:13). A good example of a chosen one in doubt of self at the time of his calling (God commissions Moses) is Moses. And Moses said unto God, Who am I, that I should go unto Pharaoh, and that I should bring forth the children of Israel out of Egypt (Exodus 3: 11)? As you see Moses doubted his self when god called on him looking through eyes of the flesh, but the Lord answered Moses. And he (The Lord) said, Certainly I will be with thee; and this shall be a token unto thee, that I have sent thee: (Exodus 3:12). This is not about you and your works is not of use, it is the present of the Lord (The Holy Spirit) that will be your compass of words and actions when it pertain to your calling from God

(The Divine One). And Moses said unto the Lord, O my Lord, I am not eloquent, neither heretofore, nor since thou hast spoken unto thy servant: but I am slow of speech, and of a slow tongue (Exodus 4:10). And the Lord said unto him, who hath made man's mouth? or who maketh the dumb, or deaf, or the seeing, or the blind? have not I the Lord (Exodus 4:11)? **Now therefore go, and I (The Lord) will be thy mouth, and teach thee what thou shalt say (Exodus 4:12).**

For ye see your calling, brethren, how that not many Wiseman after the flesh, not many mighty, not many noble, are called: (I Corinthians 1:26,29). You see in this scripture God states the ones that are called for his purpose are not chosen the way the world chooses (power, money, looks etc.) who should be in position. Even Jesus was rejected by his own (Wiseman of the flesh) they were looking for position of rank through the eye of the flesh instead of Divine Spirit from the Holy Ghost, which gives a sprit of sprit of spiritual discernment. Spiritual discernment cannot be achieved through worldly thoughts and comparison, if so they would have

11

embraced Jesus instead of shunning him. God ways are not ours ways. The world (flesh) chosen ones are due to looks, money, power, fame etc. But God hath chosen the foolish things of the world to confound the wise; and God hath chosen the weak things of the world to confound the things which are mighty; (I Corinthians 1:27). And base things of the world, and things which are despised, hath God chosen, yea, and things which are not, to bring to nought things that are: (I Corinthians 1:28). That no flesh should glory in his (Lord/Heavenly Father) presence (I Corinthians 1:29).

It is to late to retreat on the battlefield
(You have now begun your Exodus)

And Moses said unto the people, Remember this day, in which ye came out of the house of bondage; for by strength of hand the Lord brought you out from this place: (Exodus 13:3). Only God can deliver you from bondage in ways that no man shall be able to boast about. And I (The Lord) will harden Pharaoh's heart, and multiply my signs and my wonders in the land of Egypt (Exodus 7:3). And the Egyptians shall know that I am the Lord, when I stretch forth mine hand upon Egypt, and bring out the children of Israel from among them (Exodus 7:5). The Divine Farther makes Pharaoh stand firm in not letting God chosen generation go on purpose, in order to show the power and glory of the Divine and how he is always in control beyond how the opposition may look or come. This also came as training (opposition) for his chosen generation getting them ready for their Exodus out of bondage being spiritual and physical. The opposition of Pharaoh was a faith builder for the chosen generation in the Divine God/ Alpha & Omega. Alpha & Omega meaning the beginning and end the Divine God is, like he promise to be with you from the beginning and end of your opposition proven over and over in the Holy Bible through the oppositions his chosen people faced. The Lord will fight against opposition in the time of your Exodus, in only might, grace, wonders and powers that only he can bring forth in your life and like God said you will know it was only by his hand and his only at your time of Exodus (bringing out) in the wilderness of spiritual battle ground. And Moses said unto the people, Fear ye not, stand still, and see the salvation of the Lord, which he will show to you to day: for the Egyptians whom ye have seen today, ye shall see them again no more for ever (Exodus 14:13). The Lord shall fight for you, and ye shall hold your peace (Exodus 14:14).

Stand firm in conflicts of warfare

(A double minded man is unstable in all his ways (James 1:8)

Trust in the Lord at all times that he will guide and protect you, beyond how it may look or feel at troubled times. Never allow the flesh to have you in trust in the things of the world (money, human, power, fame, looks etc.). For this will cause you to be unstable on the battlefield of spiritual warfare, weaken your defense by putting your faith in things many times used by Satan but your true defense of standing firm and proven stable is with your faith in the Divine God only not wavering from one to the other.

Opposition tries to follow at your point of Exodus (breakthrough/promise land) that's how you know you are almost if not already there at your point of deliverance or blessing (Your Divine Commission).

Yea, though I walk through the valley of the shadow of death (Spiritual battle ground), I will fear no evil: for thou art with me (The promise of the Divine Alpha & Omega to be with you from the beginning and end); thy rod and thy staff they comfort me (protection against opposition) (Psalm 23:4).

Now you realize the anointing of the Divine God in and will for your life, Satan tries to follow and meet you at your every move like playing chess (spiritual warfare). Satan plan is to cause derailment on the way of your path to your commission. Satan know that you have now called in a special army of Divine reinforcement on the battlefield, once your faith became active in battle that no one or thing can come up against but you must believe always (have faith) in the Divine Father and his will and ways. If not Satan will deceive you in to thinking you have been over taken by bondage (Satan army) becoming a prisoner at war. Now lets look at how "The God of the Most High" (heaven) provided protection for his chosen people, when opposition would not let up and tried to follow at their time of Exodus.

The Divine position on the battlefield during opposition

And the angel of God, which went before the camp of Israel, removed and went behind them; and the pillar of the cloud went from before their face, and stood behind them: (Exodus 14:19). And it (The angel of God/pillar of the cloud) came between the camp of Israel; and it was a cloud and darkness to them (The oppressor), but it gave light by night to these (God chosen): so that the one came not near the other all the night (Exodus 14:20).

Pressing through opposition

You now know too much and came to far, going backward is not an option. As you see the enemy army (Satan) is on the pursuit behind you to keep you from reaching the calling and will of God in your life, as he was after God chosen people (you). Looking back as God warns us at times can be costly as it was for Lot wife while leaving the sinful city of Sodom. And it came to pass, when they had brought them forth abroad, that he said, Escape for thy life; look not behind thee, neither stay thou in all the plain; escape to the mountain, lest thou be consumed (Genesis 19:17). You must leave all your old ways of the flesh (sin) behind in order to enter The Divine. But his wife (Lot wife) looked back from behind him, and she became a pillar of salt (Genesis 19:26). Once again things of your pass (sin/ worldly things/opposition) will try to entice you to look back to return, Satan is a lie and has nothing for you but entrapment of destruction (bondage) hindering /stopping your divine calling. For if ye live after the flesh, ye shall die: but if ye through the spirit do mortify the deeds of the body, ye shall live (Romans 8:13).

Opposition being in the spiritual realm or physical comes to stop you from reaching your commission from God. Satan uses both war tactics at war, and the only true weapon of defeat is you building spiritual strength to over come both, not in the physical (flesh) things of this world. And when the devil had ended all the temptation, he departed from him for a season (Luke 4:13).

Your commission in your mission

Yea have not chosen me, but I have chosen you, and ordained you, that ye should go and bring forth fruit, and that your fruit should remain: that whatsoever ye shall ask of the father in my name, he may give it you (John 15:16). The Lord our Heavenly Father reinsures you that he chose you to be a part of The Body/ His Kingdom, meaning he knows all your flaws and set backs. Your flaws and set backs are most of the time what will bring forth the diamond out of the ruff in you, seen in many life stories in the Holy Bible. But your commission is performed and controlled by the Divine Holy Spirit not the flesh that you can control. That is why the Lord said that he have ordained you for your calling blessing you with The Holy Ghost and Holy Spirit when you start activating faith always saying: I can do all things through Christ which strengtheneth me (Philippians 4:13). I press toward the mark for the prize of the high calling of God in Christ Jesus (Philippians 3:14). And believing that any thing you lack of in your calling Our Father in Heaven will bless you with through faith and prayer. Therefore said he (Jesus) unto them, the harvest truly is great, but the labourers are few: (Luke 10:2). Go yours ways: behold, I send you forth as lambs among wolves (Luke 10:3). Satan has those that are apart of his kingdom, so you must beware as you start your mission of your commission. Spiritual warfare is always at hand so you must pray and ask The Heavenly Father for the Holy Spirit of spiritual discernment. You may come across men and women (wolves) of high and low positions to befriend you or become a part of your inner circle, with a mission of commission from Satan to lead you astray from the herd (Kingdom of God). But you have a good shepherd that promise to protect and be with you always and help you avoid the traps and snares of Satan and his army. They are a dead give away as the Lord says, Ye shall know them by their fruits do men gather grapes of thorns, or figs of thistles (Matthew 7:16)? Being aware of a person motive, lifestyle and the company they keep tells a lot about their character (Spiritual Nature). The wicked desireth the net of evil men: but the root of the righteous yieldeth fruit (Proverbs 12:12). The labour of the righteous tendeth to life: the fruit of the wicked to sin (Proverbs 10:16). I the Lord search the heart, I try the reins, even to give every man according to his ways, and according to the fruit of his doings (Jeremiah 17:10). But I will punish you according to the fruit of your doings, saith the Lord: and I will kindle a fire in the forest thereof, and it shall devour all things round about it (Jeremiah 21:14). A good tree cannot bring forth evil fruit, neither can a corrupt tree bring forth good fruit (Matthew 7:18). Wherefore by their fruits ye shall know them (Matthew 7:20). He that heareth you heareth me; and he that despiseth you despiseth me; and he that despiseth me despiseth him (The Divine God) that sent me (Luke 10:16). While performing your calling you are going to encounter people that will display a dislike of you for no reason, pray for their souls due to it is spiritual warfare of the Adversary/Satan army. This should not distract you from completing your mission of commission; Satan knows that your calling is a threat to weaken his army by saving souls from his bondage. But into whatever city ye enter, and they receive you not, go your ways out into the streets of the same, and say (Luke

10:10), Even the dust of your city, which cleaveth on us, we do wipe off against you: (Luke 10:11). This is you praying for their souls and yours that the dwelling and bondage Satan is trying to have possession over them spiritually, will be and loosed and casted out back to Hades (Hell). And no longer have power over their souls (spirit) or dwellings around them or you, hindering evil spirits from following you. And he turned him unto his disciples, and said privately, Blessed are the eyes which see the things that ye see: (Luke 10:23). For I tell you, that many prophets and kings have desired to see those things which ye see, and have not seen them; and to hear those things which ye hear, and have not heard them (Luke 10:24). Jesus is speaking of God chosen people (you), that he (God) only allows his Divine Spirit to visit and communicate his wisdom and ways with spiritually. Trust in the Lord with all thine heart; and lean not unto thine own understanding (Proverbs 3:5). In all thy ways acknowledge him, and he shall direct thy paths (Proverbs 3:6). Anything that may be at need or not yet revealed to you during your mission of commission, pray to the Lord for the wisdom and spirit of discernment, but at all times make sure your motive is in line with his (God) will if not the results are the following: Ye ask, and receive not, because ye ask amiss, that ye may consume it upon your lusts (James 4:3). But praying that God "Divine Will" be done and shown at all times results: Likewise the Spirit also helpeth our infirmities: for we know not what we should pray for as we ought: but the Spirit itself maketh intercession for us with groanings which cannot be uttered (Romans 8:26). Now knowing that you are now delegated, called to position of rank in the Divine Army/Body of the Divine Kingdom to study and spread the gospel (Word of the Lord). Our Heavenly Father/Priest will show and direct you, by anointing you with The Holy Ghost, Divine Word and guidance of The Holy Spirit, of what you must also speak and write. Feed the flock of God which is among you, taking the oversight thereof, not by constraint, but willingly; not for filthy lucre, but of a ready mind; (I Peter 5:2). A man's heart deviseth his way: but the Lord directeth his steps (Proverbs 16:9). Commit thy works unto the Lord, and thy thoughts shall be established (Proverbs 16:3). Your position has now been moved to the frontline on the battlefield (spiritual warfare), and you must learn to read and put to action blueprints of battle plans, meaning Holy Scriptures.

WRITING WITH DIVINE GUIDANCE

--------------------------------- ⟨◈⟩ ---------------------------------

The Lord gave the word: great was the company of those that published it (Psalm 68:11).

Creating a battle plan

No matter what your commission of divine mission consist of, whether it be musical, teaching, leading, preaching, counseling, etc., you must know how to break down and present the message needed personally or in a group setting. In any battle plan you must research, brainstorm, organize, strategize and write according to the battle. The battle is Spiritual Warfare, the weapons Divine Scriptures, victory in stages of battle is writing with Divine Guidance.

Research of the kingdom of Satan (demonic spirits/ soldiers of Lucifer)

.... Lest Satan should get an advantage of us: for we are not ignorant of his devices (II Corinthians 2:11).

Discerning of spirits interpretation

You need to know which demonic spirit that you are encountering on the battle field, so you can build a proper defense to counterattack against the Adversary. Be sober, be vigilant, because your adversary the devil, as a roaring lion, walketh about, seeking whom he may devour (I Peter 5:8). Put on the whole armour (Divine Word) of God, that ye may be able to stand against the wiles of the devil. (Ephesians 6:11)

Satan is always looking to send his demonic spirits (soldiers) to put an attack on souls that may not know how to fight in spiritual warfare or give in to him willing. And the Lord said unto Satan, Whence comest thou? Then Satan answered the Lord, and said, from going to and fro in the earth, and from walking up and down in it (Job 1:7) Satan strategizing an attack. The field (Battle field) is the world; the good seed are the children of the (Divine) Kingdom; but the tares are the children of the wicked one (Satan) (Matthew 13:38). Thou therefore endure hardness, as a good soldier of Jesus Christ. No man that warreth entangleth himself with the affairs of this life; that he may please him who hath chosen him to be a soldier (II Timothy 2:3-4). Love not the world, neither the things that are in the world. If any man love the world, the love of the Father is not in him. For all that is in the world, the lust of the flesh, and the lust of the eyes, and the pride of life, is not of the Father, but is of the world (I John 2:15-16).

When you allow yourself to love and be controlled by the things of this world, you are opening your soul up to the bondage of Satan. The bondage Satan entraps you with is the demonic spirit that he cast into your life, to direct your character to the will of the Adversary. Spiritual warfare is the only way to rid of any form of demonic spirit that has entered your life that is why you must study and learn to present the word of our Holy Father. This is the only weapon (Divine Scriptures) that is victorious in this form of battle, showing you different war tactics to cast out demonic spirits of different numbers and natures. The Divine Scriptures also prepare you for a counter attack against demonic spirits that has appeared to have been defeated, but lay deep in the trenches to sneak attack your soul with a revised and stronger demonic battle plan. When the unclean spirit is gone out of a man, he walketh through dry places, seeking rest, and findeth none.

Then he saith, I will return into my house (soul) from whence I came out; and when he is come, he findeth it empty, swept, and garnished.

Then goeth he and taketh with himself seven other spirits more wicked than himself and they enter in and dwell there: And the last state of that man is worse than the first... (Matthew 12:43-45). As you see the demonic spirit tries to reenter the last place (soul) of dwelling, only in order to be worst than what it appeared before. For that reason that is why you must completely die to the things and ways of sin that opened your soul to Satan, you must study and live by the prewritten battle plan (Holy Scriptures) the Divine Father has given you. In it God will reveal the traps and snares Satan set while in performance of your commission or everyday life.

The nature of attack

Satan tactics and nature of attack comes from many different realms of your everyday life. These realms Satan try to place you under his bondage may consist being personally, socially and most of all the starting point spiritually. Your spiritual state is what decides your soul defense, which is why the method of battle is spiritual warfare. Being naïve to the way the Adversary fights on the battlefield and how to discern the demonic spirit, allows Satan to control the battle according to his will.

Discernment of demonic presence and state

Possession: demonized spirits has taken control of a person soul, ether it be willing by occult practices of séances (witch, shaman, psychic, demonic worship etc.) Beloved, believe not every spirit whether they are of God: because many false prophets are gone out into the world (I John 4:1). Or unwilling brought on by living a sinful (worldly) lifestyle (thoughts and actions).

Obsession: person having demonic motives and strong interest of demonic activity, that open doors for satanic spirits a place of dwelling and bondage (possession).

Oppression: demonic spirits that brings negative thoughts, that causes a state of mind rebellious of the word (scriptures) of the Divine God. Conflicting with your faith, calling and God will for your life and those around you. A bondage that is depressive to the soul leading to sin.

Brainstorming for weapons of war

But God hath revealed them unto us by His Spirit: for the Spirit searcheth all things, yea, the deep things of God (I Corinthians 2:10). . . . opened He their understanding that they might understand the scriptures (Luke 24:45). All Scripture is given by inspiration of God, and is profitable for doctrine, for reproof, for correction, for instruction in righteousness (Spiritual Warfare): (II Timothy 3:16-17). Now we have received, not the spirit of the world, but the spirit which is of God; that we might know the things that are freely given to us of God (I Corinthians 2:12). Which things also we speak, not in the words which man's wisdom teacheth, but which the Ho'ly Ghost teacheth; comparing spiritual things with spiritual (I Corinthians 2:13). But the natural man receiveth not the things of the Spirit of God: for they are foolishness unto him: neither can he know them, because they are spiritually discerned (I Corinthians 2:14). But we speak the wisdom of God in a mystery, even the hidden wisdom, which God ordained before the world unto our glory: (I Corinthians 2:7). That your faith should not stand in the wisdom of men, but in the power of God (I Corinthians 2:5).

God given weapons for his chosen soldiers

(Must except his Divine Spirit to operate)
Old Testament 39 books THE BOOKS OF THE LAW, THE BOOKS OF HISTORY, THE BOOKS OF POETRY, THE BOOKS OF PROPHECY
New Testament 27 Books THE GOSPELS, THE BOOK OF HISTORY, LETTERS, PROPHECY

Personal battle

If we live in the (Divine) Spirit, let us also walk in the (Divine) Spirit (Galatians 5:25).

All your ways must be pleasing and in the alignment of the will of God, if not just engaging in small acts of sinful behavior can contaminate and surrender the whole spirit under demonic bondage, like leaven in bread. A little leaven leaveneth the whole lump (Galatians 5:9). But be ye doers of the word, and not hearers only, deceiving your own selves (James 1:22).

Social battle

I Peter: spiritual warfare from outside the church, from those that has not accepted their part in The Body (Kingdom of God).

II Peter: spiritual warfare from those that claim to be a part of The Body (Kingdom of God).

Supernatural battle

Finally, my brethren, be strong in the Lord, and in the power of his might (Ephesians 6:10).

Put on the whole armor (Word) of God, that ye may be able to stand against the wiles of the devil (Ephesians 6:11).

Names to call on when distressed under enemy fire (Spiritual Warfare)

Jehovah-Shammah: "The Lord is there" Ezekiel 48:35
Jehovah-Jireh: "The Lord who provides" Genesis 22:14
Jehovah-Ra'ah: "The Lord my shepherd" Psalms 23:1
Jehovah-Nissi: "The Lord our banner" Exodus 17:8-15
Jehovah-Shalom: "The Lord our peace" Judges 6:24
Jehovah-Rapha: "The Lord that healeth" Exodus 15:26
Jehovah-Tsidkenu: "The Lord our righteousness" Jeremiah 23:6

Brainstorming a Battle Plan

Search the scriptures; for in them ye think ye have eternal life: (John 5:39)

But the comforter, which is the Holy Ghost, whom the Father will send in my name, He shall teach you all things, and bring all things to your remembrance, whatsoever I have said unto you (John 14:26).

Knowing who, what and why a scripture was given at a particular time or to a person, gives insight of what spiritual battle was being dealt with and what weapon of God truth (medicine) delivered the person from the state of bondage they were experiencing. For I will restore health unto thee, and I will heal thee of thy wounds, saith the Lord.... (Jeremiah 30:17). Brainstorming this way you should be able to come up with a plan for deliverance from the enemy (Devil camp), when it comes to handling personal or social matters as seen many times used in the Bible by the Lord chosen generation to heal and deliver those that was caught in some type of demonic bondage while under spiritual warfare. A on going battle that you and others fight everyday and second in this lifetime starting with your thoughts that Satan tries to control. In most battles people protect and fight with guns and others man made weapons, which has proven to fail or be used against its owner. But God has equipped his chosen with a weapon that no man of sinful (worldly) nature, devil or demon can over power in war when used right, meaning righteously in the power and will of the Divine God. That is why Our Heavenly Father trains us through his comforter The Holy Ghost, to ordain you and The Holy Spirit to guide you giving discernment of his Holy Word the Scriptures of The Bible. Discernment and wisdom on how to build a battle plan for you and others in daily life, which is spiritual warfare.

While brainstorming study as much you can about the person or persons the scripture was written for, such as lifestyle, name (meaning), place or city of living, generational family etc. This will give more insight of why and what type of spiritual warfare the person was going through. By doing so you will learn to evaluate and organize, what scriptures may apply to you or persons in need that might be battling a situation alike or similar, this will be the starting point of your battle plan.

Also learn and study every book and its meaning, each book has its own unique meaning concerning what way God dealt with those in that book, and carried out his Divine Battle Plan for his kingdom "The Body". Study each scripture that pertains to your subject of spiritual warfare, this can be done with the aid of a bible concordance. Then the Holy Spirit will direct your path for the correct organization, to set up your weapons of spiritual warfare on the battlefield.

Organization for Battle

Organizing the scriptures found concerning your subject of spiritual warfare is best done by, gathering all main points and key words stated in the verses of scriptures then summarizing them. Summarizing each scripture (verse) according to stages and deliverance that God revealed through the loosing of bondage. The order of different stages and deliverance chosen scriptures will be according to the battle at hand. You will be lead by the Holy Spirit in which way to organize an effect battle plan. Once all scriptures are in place you are now ready to strategize a divine attack against a demonic attack.

Victorious by Strategy

Now knowing the works of the Adversary and his army, you can identify his attack and next move. By identifying his weapon of spiritual warfare you have already gained controlled over his source of power. Now you must be doers of his word not just studying it. Preach the word; (II Timothy 4:2) do the work of an evangelist, make full proof of thy ministry (II Timothy 4:5). And these things you must do according to the divine commission God has called you to, whether it be teaching, counseling, writing, musical or mentoring etc. in your personal circle and in forms of outreach. Strategizing in these ways has always been proven victorious in many ways; even blessing and delivering souls out of bondage (Exodus) you may not be aware of near and far as it has done for you (In Jesus name claim your Exodus). You are now delegated by God to deliver souls on the battlefield out of the bondage of Satan army (demonic spirits). ...Out of the house of bondage; for by strength of hand the Lord brought you out from this place: (Exodus 13:3).

Now therefore go, and I (Lord/ The most High) will be with thy mouth, and teach thee what thou shalt say (Exodus 4:12).

SOUL REVELATION

For the perfecting of the saints, for the work of the ministry, for the edifying of the body of Christ: (Ephesians 4:12). The Lord exposing your soul gives insight showing you what attacks of bondage the devil is implementing. This is a form of training (soul revelation) allows you to discern spirits in others also in need of deliverance (perfecting saints). While doing so you will also help prepare them to enter their position (ministry) in the battlefield of spiritual warfare. And he (The Divine Father) gave some, apostles; and some, prophets; and some, evangelists; and some, pastors and teachers; (Ephesians 4:11). All these different ranks on the battlefield is to edify and unify "The Body" which is God Holy Kingdom, also including any other gifts or talents that one has that can bring praise and glory to "The Body". Soul revelation is God form of spiritual correction to bring out those good things the Lord put in you, just as we would do with our own children. For whom the Lord loveth he correcteth; even as a father the son in whom he delighteth (Proverbs 3:12). For whom the Lord loveth he chasteneth, and scourgeth every son whom he receiveth. If ye endure chastening, God dealeth with you as with sons; for what son is he whom the father chasteneth not? (Hebrews 12:6,7). The Lord only chastise his chosen generation out of love, to bring them closer into his presence and place of dwelling knowing the gift he have for you and instilled in you.

I KNEW YOU IN THE WOMB

(…I do nothing of myself; but as my Father hath taught me, I speak these things (John 8:28)

Before I formed thee in the belly I knew thee; and before thou camest forth out of the womb I sanctified thee, and I ordained thee a prophet unto the nations (Jeremiah 1:5). Then said I, Ah, Lord God! behold, I cannot speak: for I am a child (Jeremiah 1:6).

The Lord warns in your time of spiritual warfare Satan (name meaning liar) will try to deceive you into to thinking God did not call (rank position) you into his Divine Army. Telling you lies that you are not qualified to meet the standards of your mission in commission. Looking at your past sins, set backs or who and what you know is the demonic spirit of deception that can cause doubt and confusion, do to self reliance other than relying on the word and promise of God to ordain you for call to duty in his kingdom "The Body". The Lord reinsures you by telling you he knew you when you was in the womb of your mother before anyone else even knew you existed, like Jesus in Mary womb, and like Jesus all his children have a calling that he has ordained and made the divine will for their (your) life. This divine will is of the Lord gifts and doing, no man can anoint you that is why he said he will guide and give you direction on where to go and what to say on the battlefield

(The World), through the Holy Ghost and Holy Spirit. But the Lord said unto me, Say not, I am a child: for thou shalt go to all that I shall send thee, and whatsoever I command thee thou shalt speak (Jeremiah 1:7). Be not afraid of their faces: for I am with thee to deliver thee, saith the Lord (Jeremiah 1:8). Above all, taking the shield of faith, wherewith ye shall be able to quench all the fiery darts of the wicked (Ephesians 6:16). For by grace are ye saved, through faith…(Ephesians 2:8). So then faith cometh by hearing, and hearing by the word of God (Romans 10:17). Then the Lord put forth his hand, and touched my mouth, And the Lord said unto me, Behold, I have put my words in thy mouth (Jeremiah 1:9). Like Jesus… I (you) will open my (your) mouth in parables; I (you) will utter things which have been kept secret from the foundation of the world (Matthew 13:35).

Positions at action in Spiritual Warfare (Take your position on the Battlefield)

For as we have many members in one body, and all members have not the same office: So we, being many, are one body in Christ, and every one members one of another. Having then gifts differing according to the grace that is given to us…let us wait on our ministering…he that teacheth, on teaching (Romans 12:4-7). Accepting your Divine Calling, is serving God as a soldier in his army according to your gift, predestine by the will of God. Your gift is unique and is not meant to copy or mimic anyone in any form or fashion. That is why God made you unlike anyone else down to your fingerprint, like your fingerprint identifies you and only who you are as the same should be for your walk in ministry. But there are titles that Holy Ghost and Holy Spirit will reveal to you as your Divine Calling, better understood when knowledgeable about them.

ORIGIN OF THE BODY (PERSONAL FOUNDATION/ EVANGELISM)

The genesis (origin) and personal foundation of any ministry starts with the evangelistic conversion process of deliverance of the soul from the bondage of (Sin) Lucifer, to accept the deliver and saver" The Divine God" resulting in a new way of life from sin the ways of the world into living day by day in a way that is lead and focused on the word of "The Most High" and his divine will.

Evangelist: sharing the word of God with unbelievers, in order to save their soul from sin (death) by accepting God Almighty (everlasting life). Soul converting a position held in spiritual warfare by Jesus and Apostle Paul, two Evangelist of some of the main stories of evangelism in the bible. Also leading and training others in ways they should acknowledge and obtain their will of God in "The Body".

Apostle: a seed planter, developer and organizer of places of worship (Missionary).

Pastor: a shepherd over the church and God sheep (believers).

Prophet: inspirational speaker having the divine gift to hear God given communication (messages).

Teacher: the ability to understand and teach others about the bible and the word of God, for soul converting and everyday living.

Do not be limited only to these ways of ministry, God give many others ways in "The Body" to perform his will such as music, mentoring, prayer, donating time or funds to ministry or those in need etc. Pray and God will speak to your soul in all the ways you are gifted for ministry in "The Body".

CAST YOUR NET

(Evangelist)

And Jesus, walking by the sea of Galilee, saw two brethren, Simon called Peter, and Andrew his brother, casting a net into the sea: for they were fishers (Matthew 4:18). And he saith unto them, Follow me, and I will make you fishers of men (Matthew 4:19).

One of Jesus main goals was the conversion of souls, by teaching about the Divine Father, and the way you should inner act in everyday life and with others. By casting your net causing souls to be converted and drawn into

"The Kingdom of God" like a fisher net at sea. Again, the kingdom of heaven is like unto a net, that was cast into the sea, and gathered of every kind: (Matthew 13:47). Which, when it was full, they drew to shore, and sat down, and gathered the good into vessels, but cast the bad away (Matthew 13:48). Then saith he unto his disciples, The harvest truly is plenteous, but the laborers are few; (Matthew 9:37). The Lord plan is that no one should perish, many will reject you and the word of God as they did Jesus also, that is why going to and from you must always seek the "Heavenly Father" through communication. Pray ye therefore the Lord of the harvest, that he will send forth laborers into his harvest (Matthew 9:38). In doing so you rid of any demonic spirits that is present and causing bondage over the soul from divine conversion. And when he called unto him his twelve disciples, he gave them power against unclean spirits, to cast them out, (Matthew 10:1). But watch thou in all things, endure afflictions, do the work of an evangelist, make full proof of thy ministry (2 Timothy 4:5). For the perfecting of the saints, for the work of the ministry, for the edifiying of the body of Christ: (Ephesians 4:12). This is spiritual warfare and your goal like Jesus is converting souls (the saints) to become soldiers in "The Body" God "Divine Kingdom", through evangelism the origin of spiritual soul training ministry in every area of ministry.

Evangelistic Conversion

Apostle Paul also know as Saul use to kill Christians until a bright light knocked him down and blinded him saying, I am Jesus whom you are persecuting (Act 9:4-5). The Holy Spirit led him to a place to have his sight restored by a believer that evangelized to him converting his soul to commission as missionary to become a great seed planter of churches (an Apostle) and Evangelistic. Apostle Paul life recordings can be found in the chapters of Acts in the Bible, and his actions with many churches.

MUSTARD SEED & LEAVEN

The Kingdom of heaven is like to a grain of mustard seed, which a man took, and sowed in his field: (Matthew 13:31). You must evangelize in order to convert souls, speaking the word of God to someone and teaching them the ways to do the same to others is planting a seed in the field (the world). He that soweth the good seed is the Son of man; (Matthew 13:37). When Jesus planted seeds he spoke in parables simple stories that could be considered small talk but look at the revelation and power in soul conversion that came from it. Another parable put he (Jesus) forth unto them, saying, the kingdom of heaven is likened unto a man which sowed good seed in his field: (Matthew 13:24). But while men slept, his enemy (Satan) came and sowed tares among the wheat, and went his way (Matthew 13:25). Satan also sows seed, knowing the power it has even little by little seed planting. Usually when Satan knows a Divine seed (God Word) has been planted he will try to up root it, to hinder a soul from being converted to keep it in bondage. Sending demonic forces to attack your inner and outer state, that is why you must research the kingdom of Satan for knowledge of spiritual discernment as I talked about earlier in my chapter of "Writing with Divine Guidance". Praying and embracing the word of God will give you the right weaponry needed, because the word of God always ignite spiritual warfare, causing the Adversary to ambush an attack as Jesus warned us. Think not that I am come to send peace on earth: I came not to send peace, but a sword (spiritual warfare) (Matthew

10:34). But when the blade was sprung up, and brought forth fruit, then appeared the tares also (Matthew 13:26). The field is the world; the good seed are the children of the kingdom; but the tares are the children of the wicked one; (Matthew 13:38). The enemy that sowed them is the devil; (Matthew 13:39). A good tree cannot bring forth evil fruit, neither can a corrupt tree bringeth forth good fruit (Matthew 7:18). And have no fellowship with the unfruitful works of darkness, but rather reprove them (Ephesians 6:11).

Even once you have learned to live in the Divine spirit apart from the ways of the world, there will still be those who claim to be of a Divine spirit but only there to derail you from your walk in the "Kingdom of the Divine God". But only so long can they really stand in the word of God before the truth will be revealed. The truth the word of God and a lie of deceit of Satan cannot stand as one and will soon be shifted apart like the wheat and tare. Yea a sword shall pierce through thy own soul also, that the thoughts of many hearts may be revealed (Luke 2:35). For the word of God is quick, and powerful, and shaper than any two edged sword, piercing even to the dividing asunder of soul and spirit, and of the joints and marrow, and is a discerner of the thoughts and intents of the heart (Hebrew 4:12). The double edge sword (God Word) will be a discerner now as you witness soul converting through evangelism and later in the revelation of spiritual warfare. And he had in his right hand seven stars: and out of his mouth went a sharp two edged sword: (Revelation 1:16).

You must tend to the field

That seed cultivated daily in by speaking the word of God to self and others, is the start of a divine harvest growth process. When divinely nourished, by a word or verse here and there among the world may not seem to be much but, which indeed is the least of all seeds: but when it is grown, it is the greatest among herbs, (Matthew 13:32). The kingdom of heaven is like unto leaven, which a woman took, and hid in three measures of meal, till the whole was leavened (Matthew 13:33). Like leaven the word of God is so powerful people do not realize it do not take much to effect the whole soul, as long as it is received and taken in an effect will reap from it.

THY KINGDOM COME

And as ye go, preach, saying, the kingdom of heaven is at hand (Matthew 10:7). Letting them know there is a on going spiritual battle and you are going to take part in it by being under the bondage of Satan or putting on the whole armor of God. Wherefore be ye not unwise, but understanding what the will of the Lord is (Ephesians 6:17). Accepting every door that opens and that are shut, while not leaning to knowledge of this world, but now leaning on the promise of God that all things work together for good for those chosen as part of "The Body" his "Divine Kingdom". It will all work according to his perfect plan concerning your mission in commission (calling) as you see from the stories of those like you in the bible. And ye shall seek me, and find me, when ye shall search for me with all your heart (Jeremiah 29:13). And all things, whatsoever ye shall ask in prayer, believing, ye shall receive (Matthew 21:22). At the start of your day and journey in ministry always consult with the Lord in prayer. Thy kingdom come. Thy will be done in earth, as it is in heaven (Matthew 6:10) in Jesus name AMEN (SO BE IT). In praying this daily prayer opens your soul, allowing humbling to thelema and boulema which both ties you into God voice hearing his will.

GUIDE MY FOOTSTEPS

A man's heart deviseth his way: but the Lord directeth his steps (Proverbs 16:9). In all thy ways acknowledge him, and he shall direct thy paths (Proverbs 3:6).

Ask, and it shall be given you; seek, and ye shall find; knock, and it shall be opened unto you: (Matthew 7:7). But seek ye first the kingdom of God, and his righteousness; and all these things shall be added unto you (Matthew 6:33). As you follow and live by the word of God you shall reap God given gifts and blessings that no man or demon can steal or diminish from your spirit, as long as you walk in the Divine Spirit.

And they were all filled with the Holy Ghost, and began to speak with other tongues, as the spirit gave them utterance (Acts 2:4). And these signs shall they cast out devils; they shall speak with new tongues; (Mark 16:17).

BIBLICAL INSIGHTS

Prophets in the Old Testament acted as interpreters and messenger of God word and future plans. As part of The Old Testament there are 16 books that are named after the prophet concerning that book. I recommend reading those books to see the many different ways God spoke and communicated with his divine chosen as individuals like he deals with you and others everyday. The Apocalyptic prophetic books of the bible concerning signs and wonders of divine judgment, the Lord tells about the ending of this world in which you are preparing for now while reading this book and taking heed to your part (spiritual warfare) in the "Divine Kingdom" "The Body" are the book of Daniel and Revelation. End time (soul revelation) will bring forth many false prophets claiming to be of the Divine Kingdom and that has trained under the leadership of a demonic spirit from Satan of entrapment. Beware of false prophets, which come to you in sheep's clothing, but inwardly they are ravening wolves (Matthew 7:15).

King of Kings Lord of Lords

The Lord never intended for his people to be ruled under a manmade kingdom, such as under ruler ship of a King (1 & 2 Kings /Bible). The system of the world is to give power and authority to man (a person of the flesh) that in most cases do not acknowledge the "Divine God" and his guidance. That is why the Lord Jehovah showed his anger many times in the bible even now in our present days of life. His wrath shown because many souls are led astray by leaders of the world that compromise or adapt in ways of the world, instead of standing strong with faith in the divine word and obedience to the Lord do's and don'ts of life. Kings of the world reveal their Lord and belief by their ways and the fruit of their labor, that conflict with the divine spirit training in spirituality. Kings and their kingdoms lead by the ways of the world (flesh) produce tare among the wheat in the field (the world) like shown in scriptures of the bible. These shall make war with the Lamb, and the Lamb shall overcome them: for he is Lord of Lords, and King of Kings: and they that are with him are called, and chosen, and faithful (Revelation 17:14). Last but not least he is the only true leadership needed in life promising to be your Jehovah-jireh (Genesis 22:14) in every area of need.

Events

The ways of God and the events caused by his actions in the bible show that everything happens for a reason and according to his will even in your everyday journey. And the Lord promise is that all things works out for the good that are his chosen, and are within the purpose of the Lord will. But in order for this to be fulfilled and manifest in your life, you must remain within his divine spiritual will. And not wavering to your own or somebody else will that may not be God true predestine plan for your individual life, meaning walking and living according to his word and will along with prayer seeking him at all times and in every situation. Any actions of the flesh (sin) emotionally or physically can discourage or hinder your spiritual growth and anointing, leading you to seek the will of the flesh not the Lord. Many have reaped great sorrow, lost or even death, by following their own will as shown in many events of the bible and even events personally or socially you may know of. But there are also those that received the great reward of following God will for their life, it being the calling of their part in his "Divine Kingdom" "The Body". Events good and bad in the bible are training tools as you evangelize, all relating to soul conversion or rebellion to convert. As you plant the good seed (God Word) to harvest (convert souls), you can mention accordingly as inspirational examples from biblical events.

Tribes

Priests hood: the holy tribe of the 12 tribes the Levites, God ordained over his tabernacle and divine duties.

Personal holiness: was to be the focus as well for others

The tribe of Levi descendants of Aaron the brother of Moses

Levites people in charge of god tabernacle the Ark of the Covenant

Duties of the priests and Levites were offering and sacrifices and how should be made accordingly.

The books Leviticus and Deuteronomy are consider the books of God laws for remaining in the divine spirit, given to his chosen to keep them from spiritual bondage and entrapment of the snare from the demonic adversary kingdom. When these two books are studied it gives more spiritual insight on the how and why many fell and fall during spiritual warfare in the bible and everyday life, and how you and others prevail in spiritual warfare by obedience to the laws of the Divine God. Who by just his name can protect and provide, even the demons tremble from fear of his Divine Holy name.

Fear none of those things which thou shalt suffer: behold, the devil shall cast

And that they may recover themselves out of the snare of the devil, who are taken captive by him at his will. (II Timothy 2:26)

some of you into prison, that ye may be tried... (Revelation 2:10)

Names Of God

EL SHADDAI / GOD ALMIGHTY
YAHWEH / Y-H-W-W
ADONAY / THE LORD
JEHOVAH / A COMBINATION OF Y-H-W-H & ADONAY

Jehovah-jireh promise to be our (provider) in always blessing us with Jehovah-shalom (peace) even in times of trouble and opposition through Jehovah-shalom (peace) and Jehovah-tsidkenu (our righteousness) he Jehovah-rophe (heals) our land of sin when Jehovah-rohi the (Divine shepherd) guides spiritual conversion as Jehovah-m'kaddesh (sanctifies) us with Jehovah-nissi (banner) of Jehovah-shammah God is (omnipresent /there always) in Holy Spirit.

God is a spirit: and they that worship him must worship him in spirit and in truth (John 4:24). But ye are not in the flesh, but in the spirit, if so be that the spirit of god dwell in you. Now if any man have not the spirit of Christ, he is none of His (Romans 8:9).

The Spirit of the Lord is upon me, because He hath anointed me to preach the gospel to the poor; He hath sent me to heal the brokenhearted, to preach deliverance to the captives, and recovering of sight to the blind, to set at liberty them that are bruised (Luke 4:18).

By the Holy Spirit the Lord works through you as an intercessor to teach and convert souls from death of demonic bondage, to deliverance to walk and live in the Divine Spirit as his chosen generation. In no form or fashion by the works of the flesh can any state of soul conversion be performed, but only by the Divine Spirit that come from Jehovah (The Most High God). The Lord anointing must rest within you and it will be evident of his presence, through it he (The Lord) not man will be glorified. He shall not speak of himself (John 16:13). But ye shall receive power after that the Holy Ghost is come upon you... (Acts 1:8). For the prophecy came not in old time by the will of man but holy men of God spake as they were moved by the Holy Ghost. (II Peter 1:21). Not by might, nor by power, but by my spirit saith the Lord (Zechariah 4:6).

Obedient to the Divine Word/ Not Sinful Nature

(Grieve the Spirit doing what the Holy Spirit do not want you to do)

And grieve not the Holy Spirit of God, whereby ye are sealed unto the day of

Redemption (Ephesians 4:30). Grieving the Holy Spirit by sinful nature or rebellion can hinder and strip your anointing because the Holy Spirit can not dwell in a unclean soul, only to return when the soul has been divinely converted accepting to divine will and living. The degree and nature of the Holy Spirit returning is between the personal relationship with the Lord and person, being the Divine God can only direct the Holy Spirit not the power of man (flesh). Many people of today and even in the bible have lost their Divine Spirit (The Holy Spirit) from results of sinful acts or rebellion later reconverting through true repentance to receive the Holy Spirit but only by the will of God.

The Holy Spirit is **omnipotent,** powerful in all ways (Psalms 62:11) its power is displayed in the soul conversion process. Many times the Lord will anoint one person to be his intercessor like he did with Jesus to convert souls of thousands or even millions in the matter of seconds just by his Divine Word. You see that the Lord has used many other divine chosen in the bible and even today to carry out soul saving (converting), as he is doing with you just by becoming an acting part of

"The Body". In doing so the Holy Spirit is **omnipresent,** everywhere (Psalms 139:7), which what makes it possible to convert souls in more places than one, even places you have never seen or been just by your ministry. The Holy Spirit will lead and guide you into what to say and do in any situation because the Holy Spirit is **omniscient**, know the unknown and known (I Corinthians 2:10-11) a perfect weapon on the battlefield of spiritual warfare and preparation of the Rapture.

THE RAPTURE

By the Holy Spirit you are to be converting souls from one place to another, as Jesus did when he walked the earth and his commission when he returns. Saving souls by deliverance from demonic bondage and destruction by Divine deliverance into Jehovah Divine Kingdom for perfect and everlasting life nonexistence of death. Meanwhile you are to take part in the preparation of Rapture performing soul conversion, only those souls that has been divinely converted and are part of "The Body" will have their name written in **The Book of Life** assigned for deliverance to the Divine Kingdom when the judgment of "The Most High God" is at hand.

The Rapture promise for his chosen generation (The Day Of The Lord)
I Thessalonians 4:13-18

Many will not take heed and will not be happy that were in rebellion against the Divine soul conversion process and will be subject to tribulation of this corrupt (sinful) world when "The Day of the Lord" comes. Behold, he cometh with clouds; and every eye shall see him, and they also which pierced him: and all kindreds of the earth shall wail because of him. Even so, Amen (Revelation 1:7). No one shall escape the judgment of the Lord and the Lord wishes no one should parish. And I give unto them eternal life; and they shall never perish, neither shall any man pluck them out of my hand

(John 10:28). So your commission is God will to save and reveal his heavenly kingdom to them now by over succeeding the lies that Satan (meaning liar) tells causing rebellion to the Divine Word for souls not converting now. Later is too late and no man knows the timing of God. But the day of the Lord will come as a thief in the night; in the which the heavens shall pass away with a great noise, and the elements shall melt with fervent heat, the earth also and the works that are therein shall be burned up (II Peter 3:10). By Spiritual Warfare you must save the wounded, lost and bondage souls, those that have sold their soul to Satan for the false and corrupt things of this world. Again, the devil taketh him up into an exceeding high mountain, and showeth him all the kingdoms of the world, and the glory of them; (Matthew 4:8). And saith unto him (Jesus), All these things will I give thee, if thou wilt fall down and worship me (Matthew 4:9). No man can serve two masters: for either he will hate the one, and love the other; or else he will hold to the one, and despise the other. Ye cannot serve God and mammon (Matthew 6:24). Therefore I say unto you, Take no thought for your life, what ye shall eat, or what ye shall drink; nor yet for your body, what ye shall put on. Is not the life more than meat, and the body than raiment (Matthew 6:25)?

Behold the fowls of the air: for they sow not, neither do they reap, nor gather into barns; yet your heavenly Father feedeth them. Are ye not much better than they (Matthew 6:26)? Lay not up for yourselves treasures upon earth, where moth and rust doth corrupt, and where thieves break through and steal: (Matthew 6:19). But lay up for your selves treasures in heaven, where neither moth nor rust doth corrupt, and where thieves do not break through nor steal: (Matthew 6: 20). For where your treasure is, there will your heart be also (Matthew 6:21). That is why evangelizing to souls lost and under demonic bondage (spiritual warfare), in order to cause spiritual conversion should be your main mission of focus in the battlefield (the world). No matter what type of commission (calling / ministry) you have you are to convert the dead (sin) to life (Divine living) to save their soul from Hades (Hell). Sinful living is a death sentence for the soul that can only be repelled by divine living, that promises every lasting life giving by Jehovah (The Divine Judge). And I saw the dead, small and great, stand before God; and the books were opened, and another book was opened, which is **The Book of Life**: and the dead were judged out of those things which were written in the books, according to their works (Revelation 20:12). And the sea gave up the dead which were in it; and death and hell delivered up the dead which were them: and they were judged every man according to their works (Revelation 20:13). And death and hell were cast into the lake of fire. This is the second death (Revelation 20:14). And whosoever was not found written in **The Book of Life** was cast into the lake of fire (Revelation 20:15).

Rev19: 16 Kings of Kings Lords of Lords

Kingdom Living (Mind Set): Matthews 6:1-34 is the mind set training chapter for a new and current solider in "The Body" acting on the battlefield in spiritual warfare. I leave you to read and study this chapter when daily opposition accrues and needing to know where to look for your strength and power (spiritual ammunition) in time of need. Not searching in the ways of the world, which the Adversary uses daily as entrapment for wondering souls. As he also tried and tempted Jesus to gain control of his soul during spiritual warfare (Matthew 4:1-11), like in today world temptation set target daily for each and every person on this earth.

Positioning for Opposition

Satan knows of the Rapture and seeks to gain as many souls he can to not convert into the Divine to receive a death sentence in Hades (Hell) with him and his demonic army. But his main strategy of plan is through the ways of the world being the ways of man, which is sinful by nature. This is why encountering with an unconverted soul first result in rebellion to the Divine God, Divine word and Divine living because of the ways and thinking of man is of the flesh not the spirit. God is a spirit: and they that worship him (The Heavenly Father) must worship him in (Divine) spirit and in truth (John 4:24). And this is condemnation, that light is come into the world, and men loved darkness rather than light, because their deeds were evil (John 3: 19). For everyone that doeth evil hateth the light, neither cometh to the light, lest his deeds should be reproved (John 3:20).

This why many try to avoid the Divine Word not knowing it is really a demonic spirit that has their soul running to remain captive to a eternal death sentence.

Though all men shall be offended because of thee, yet will I never be offended (Matthew 26:33). This is standing true and committed to the delegated mission of the Heavenly Father, not giving in or surrendering because of what they or the world might think or do, if not you to will become pleaser of man instead of "The Most High God" (Jehovah) denying his "Divine Will" becoming demonically captive and lost as well (Spiritual Warfare). Verily I say unto thee, That this night, before the cock crow, thou shalt deny me thrice (Matthew 26:34). To avoid this tactic of Satan and deliver a soul under his bondage must be done by Divine Spirit not of the flesh as man and Satan (ways of the world). With men it is impossible, but not with God: for with God all things are possible (Mark 10:27).

And ye shall be hated of all men for my name's sake: but he that endureth to the end shall be saved (Matthew 10:22). And fear not them which kill the body, but are not able to kill the soul: but rather fear him which is able to destroy both soul and body in hell (Matthew 10:28) But whosoever shall deny me before men, him will I also deny before my father which is in heaven (Matthew 10:33). He that is not with me is against me; and he that gathereth not with me scattereth abroad (Matthew 12:30).

D&D (Divine vs. Demonic soul conversion)

He that findeth his life shall lose it: and he that loseth his life for my sake shall find it (Matthew 10:39). Preparation for kingdom living is soul converting from demonic to the Divine and accepting your calling and duty in the battlefield. This transformation grants your name to be written in **"The Book of Life"** for the day of Divine judgment. But you must not be as those that are so caught up in the ways of the world that refuse to be submissive to the voice of God, and try to remain in fear of their calling and leaving their old life and ways, instead of moving forward to the life God has in "The Body" (Divine Kingdom) for you. Fear is from the Devil looking from the natural eye (Flesh) instead of having Faith in God for the talent to anoint you with The Holy Ghost and guide you with The Holy Spirit he has blessed you with. And I was afraid, and went and hid thy talent in the earth: lo, there thou hast that is thine (Matthew 25:25). His Lord (Jehovah) answered and said unto him, Thou wicked and slothful servant, (Matthew 25:26)

Entering the Divine Kingdom

How hard is it for them that trust in riches to enter into the kingdom of God (Mark 10:24). Many sell their soul for riches and the fame of man in more ways than one, due to those riches of this world is not only concerning money. Materialism and the pride of man is also worldly (sinful) riches, even in the bible this sin was a great snare for many. The Blinded (in darkness / sin) by the ways of this world and its riches, Satan brings destruction in ways of murder, fornication, adultery, theft, envy, lust etc. Riches have even caused those of the Divine Generation to backslide or fall into sin, and losing track of the will of God some never returning. Then shall two be in the field; the one shall be taken, and the other left (Matthew 24:40). Not every one that saith unto me, Lord, Lord shall enter into the kingdom of heaven; but he that doeth the will of my father which is in heaven (Matthew 7:21). This is why you must beware of not becoming side tracked by the things of this world, and always is delegated to preparing souls for the Rapture as Jesus delegated through evangelizing. Watch therefore: for ye know not what hour your Lord doth come (Matthew 24:42).

Remembrance
Yours truly,

The fear of the Lord is the beginning of knowledge: but fools despise wisdom and Instruction (Proverbs 1:7). Commission in the Divine Generation to focus on the boulema (Will of God) always guided by The Holy Spirit no more by God conflicting emotions of the flesh in every part of your life. Following and planning according to the thelema of Jehovah with a converted divine out look not of the natural eye (Ways of man/ flesh). My son, walk not thou in the way with them; refrain thy foot from their path (Proverbs 1:15). "He that is not with me is against me" (Luke 11:23) **Spiritual Warfare**.

Every soul is valuable to God: "The Lord is not willing that any should perish"
(2 Peter 3:9).